Managing Editor
Mara Ellen Guckian

Editor in Chief
Karen J. Goldfluss, M.S. Ed.

Creative Director
Sarah M. Fournier

Cover Artist
Marilyn Goldberg

Illustrator
Mark Mason

Art Coordinator
Renée Mc Elwee

Imaging
Amanda R. Harter

Publisher
Mary D. Smith, M.S. Ed.

TCR 3119

Build Words

Using Base Words, Prefixes & Suffixes

miss- -ing -in
non- re-
-less -board- con-
bi- -er -ful -es
-ment

Word-building activities to improve vocabulary knowledge and reading comprehension

Teacher Created Resources

Authors
Mara Guckian and Stephanie Yang

Teacher Created Resources
12621 Western Avenue
Garden Grove, CA 92841
www.teachercreated.com

ISBN: 978-1-4206-3119-7

©2015 Teacher Created Resources
Reprinted, 2019
Made in U.S.A.

Teacher Created Resources

Table of Contents

Introduction

The dictionary defines a word as "a single distinct meaningful element of speech or writing . . ." Vocabulary is the study of words, their meanings, and proper usage.

The *Building Words* series provides students with opportunities to examine words—to see how they are put together, to define them, and to use them appropriately.

This exploration begins with a discussion of base words and roots. Compound words are explored and study expands to examine affixes—specifically prefixes and suffixes. Identifying and defining root or base words and affixes are essential skills for decoding unfamiliar words. They are skills emphasized in the Common Core State Standards across most grade levels.

This series will provide students with word decoding practice that they can use in school in order to improve reading comprehension and fluency. Students will hopefully become enamored with the study of words and become *wordsmiths*—skilled users of words.

How to Use This Book

1. Prepare a folder for each student. Explain that these are their Wordsmith Folders. They will become wordsmiths. Wordsmiths work with words to become skillful writers.

2. Add the following reference pages, card sets, and games to their folders to use as needed:

   ☐ *Dictionary Practice* template (page 6) to be copied and used as needed.

   ☐ *Common Prefixes List* (page 12)

   ☐ *Numerical Prefixes List* (page 29)

   ☐ *Common Suffixes List* (page 33)

   ☐ *Words Can Grow* template (page 58)

3. Activity pages can be done in order or pulled as needed to address specific student needs. First, review the Quick Lesson on each page with students. Discuss examples, when provided, and share other words known to match the activity or the rule. Finally, provide ample time for student wordsmiths to work independently, to do necessary research, and to share their findings with each other.

4. Establish interactive *Prefix* and *Suffix Word Walls* in the classroom in order to build enthusiasm and to encourage student engagement. Each time a student finds an appropriate prefix or suffix word, have him or her add the word and its definition to an index card and add it to the appropriate column on the wall. You might also consider having blank webs available for word studies.

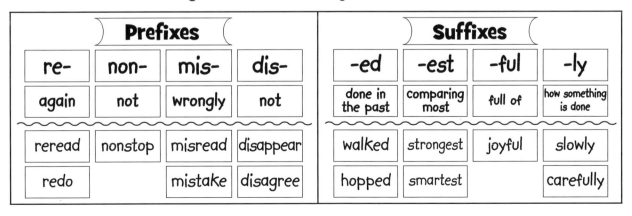

Prefixes				**Suffixes**			
re-	non-	mis-	dis-	-ed	-est	-ful	-ly
again	not	wrongly	not	done in the past	comparing most	full of	how something is done
reread	nonstop	misread	disappear	walked	strongest	joyful	slowly
redo		mistake	disagree	hopped	smartest		carefully

Common Core State Standards

The lessons and activities in *Building Words: Using Base Words, Prefixes, and Suffixes, Grade 3* meet one or more of the following Common Core State Standards. For more information about the Common Core State Standards, go to *http://www.corestandards.org/*.

Visit *http://www.teachercreated.com/standards/* for more correlations to Common Core State Standards.

Reading: Foundational Skills	Pages
ELA.RF.3.3.A Identify and know the meaning of the most common prefixes and derivational suffixes.	11–61
ELA.RF.3.3.B Decode words with common Latin suffixes.	33–61
ELA.RF.3.3.C Decode multisyllable words.	8–10
ELA.RF.3.3.D Read grade-appropriate irregularly spelled words.	52
ELA.RF.3.4.C Use context to confirm or self-correct word recognition and understanding, rereading as necessary.	All Activities
Speaking and Listening	
ELA.SL.3.1 Engage effectively in a range of collaborative discussions (one-on-one, in groups, and teacher-led) with diverse partners on *grade 3 topics and texts*, building on others' ideas and expressing their own clearly.	All Activities
ELA.SL.3.1.D Explain their own ideas and understanding in light of the discussion.	All Activities
Language	
ELA.L.3.1 Demonstrate command of the conventions of standard English grammar and usage when writing or speaking.	All Activities
ELA.L.3.1.B Form and use regular and irregular plural nouns	49–52
ELA.L.3.1.E Form and use the simple (e.g., *I walked; I walk; I will walk*) verb tenses.	37, 40, 48, 57–61
ELA.L.3.1.G Form and use comparative and superlative adjectives and adverbs, and choose between them depending on what is to be modified.	53–55
ELA.L.3.2.E Use conventional spelling for high-frequency and other studied words and for adding suffixes to base words (e.g., *sitting, smiled, cries, happiness*).	36–61
ELA.L.3.2.F Use spelling patterns and generalizations (e.g., *word families, position-based spellings, syllable patterns, ending rules, meaningful word parts*) in writing words.	All Activities
ELA.L.3.2.G Consult reference materials, including beginning dictionaries, as needed to check and correct spellings.	All Activities
ELA.L.3.4.A Use sentence-level context as a clue to the meaning of a word or phrase.	All Activities
ELA.L.3.4.B Determine the meaning of the new word formed when a known affix is added to a known word (e.g., *agreeable/disagreeable, comfortable/uncomfortable, care/careless, heat/preheat*).	All Activities
ELA.L.3.4.C Use a known root word as a clue to the meaning of an unknown word with the same root (e.g., *company, companion*).	All Activities
ELA.L.3.4.D Use glossaries or beginning dictionaries, both print and digital, to determine or clarify the precise meaning of key words and phrases.	All Activities
ELA.L.3.5.B Identify real-life connections between words and their use (e.g., describe people who are *friendly* or *helpful*).	All Activities

Alphabetizing Words

A dictionary is a great tool. It can tell you how to spell a word correctly, what part of speech it is, and what it means. Words in a dictionary are arranged alphabetically. That means that the words are arranged in the same order as the letters of the alphabet.

Astronaut comes before *bark* because the letter "Aa" comes before the letter "Bb."

Directions: Look at the list of words below and put them in alphabetical order.

glide	1. _____
observe	2. _____
arrange	3. _____
vine	4. _____
mural	5. _____
recall	6. _____

Sometimes, the words you are arranging begin with the same letter, like *signal* and *solution*. Since both of those words start with "Ss" you need to look at the second letter to help you put the words in alphabetical order. The word *signal* would come before *solution*, because "Ii" comes before "Oo."

Directions: All the words in the list below begin with the letter "Pp." Use the second letter of each word to help you put the words in alphabetical order.

print	7. _____
passage	8. _____
perform	9. _____
point	10. _____
plan	11. _____
publish	12. _____

Directions: All the words below begin with the same three letters. Can you alphabetize them?

consider	13. _____
confine	14. _____
continent	15. _____

Bonus

Explain how you alphabetized the last three words.

_____

_____

_____

Name: _____

Dictionary Practice

Directions: Look up four words in the dictionary. Find a noun, a verb, an adverb, and an adjective. Read each word entry and fill in the boxes below.

1. Word: _____

Number of syllables: _____   Part of Speech: _____

Definition: _____

_____

2. Word: _____

Number of syllables: _____   Part of Speech: _____

Definition: _____

_____

3. Word: _____

Number of syllables: _____   Part of Speech: _____

Definition: _____

_____

4. Word: _____

Number of syllables: _____   Part of Speech: _____

Definition: _____

_____

Bonus Can you use all four words in a sentence or short story? Use a separate sheet of paper or the back of this page.

Base Words or Roots?

What is the difference between a *base word* and a *root*?

This is a question that is subject to much debate and there are two main schools of thought. Many educators feel that a root is a "word part" which requires a prefix, a suffix, or both to complete it, while a base word is a complete word that can stand on it's own. Other educators feel that there is no difference and that both "root" and "base" refer to the basic, core part of a word—the part that prefixes and suffixes can be added to.

Whenever possible, stand-alone base words are used in this book. The roots found in this book are those most familiar to students at this grade level. These include *-tract*, as in *subtract*, *-scribe*, as in *describe*, and *-cite*, as in *recite*. Shape and number word roots are also included as these are common academic vocabulary. Roots will be addressed more fully in later grades.

Base Words

A **base word** is a complete word.

- Base words can stand on their own.

   (bird, cat, dog, house, butter, fly)

- Two base words can form a compound word.

   (bird + house = birdhouse; butter + fly = butterfly)

- A prefix can be added to the beginning of a base word to make a new word with a new meaning.

   (re + read = reread)

- A suffix can be added to the end of a base word to make a new word with a new meaning.

   (read + er = reader)

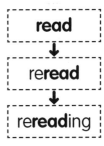

Roots

A **root** (*bio*) or **root word** (*gram*) is the very basic part of a word.

- A root does not usually stand alone.

   (cycl, uni, multi, bio, geo, tech)

- Roots can be found at the beginning, middle, or end of a word.

   (cycl → <u>cycl</u>ing, uni<u>cycl</u>e, bi<u>cycl</u>es, motor<u>cycl</u>e)

- Word families consist of words that share the same root.

   (phon → micro<u>phon</u>e, tele<u>phon</u>e, <u>phon</u>ograph)

- Some words consist of two or more roots. (<u>photograph</u>) Sometimes, one of the words is also considered a prefix. (<u>universe</u>)

- Many roots have either Greek or Latin origins.

   (Cycl is a Greek root meaning wheel. Words such as unicycle, motorcycle, and bicycle can be made using the Greek root cycl.)

   (Uni is a Latin root meaning one. Words such as unit, uniform, unite, and reunite can be made with the Latin root uni. Often, uni is also considered a prefix.)

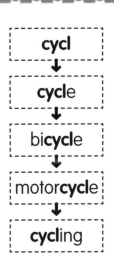

Name: _____

Make Compound Words

> **Quick Lesson**—A **compound word** is formed by combining two base words. Often, the first word describes the second word, which is the main idea.
>
> **Example:** air + plane = airplane ➜ An *airplane* is a type of vehicle that flies in the *air*.

Directions: Combine the words in the list on the left with the word **book** to make new compound words on the right.

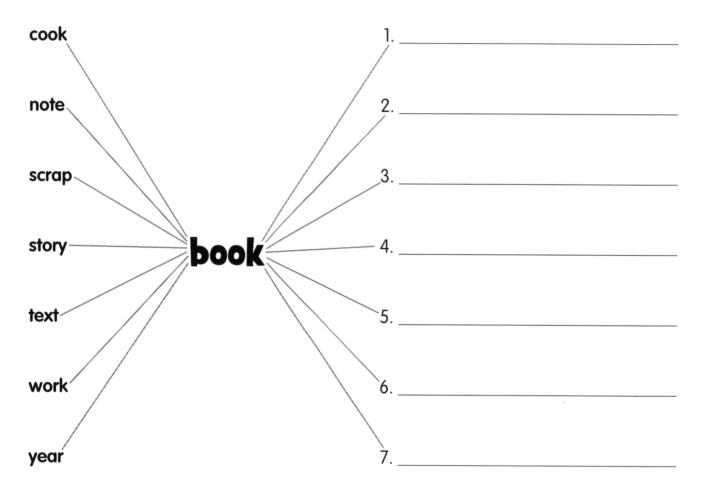

cook

note

scrap

story

text

work

year

book

1. _____

2. _____

3. _____

4. _____

5. _____

6. _____

7. _____

Directions: Write a short story using at least three of the compound words you made.

_____

_____

_____

_____

_____

Compound Word Cards

Teacher Directions

1. Prepare copies for each student group to cut out.

2. Provide snack-size, resealable bags or small containers for storage.

Student Directions

1. Work in small groups. Cut out the base word cards on the dashed lines.

2. Combine the base words cards to make compound words.

3. Write the compound words on a separate sheet of paper or create one class list.

4. Circle the compound words on the list if the first base word describes the second base word.

5. Compare the compound words with other groups.

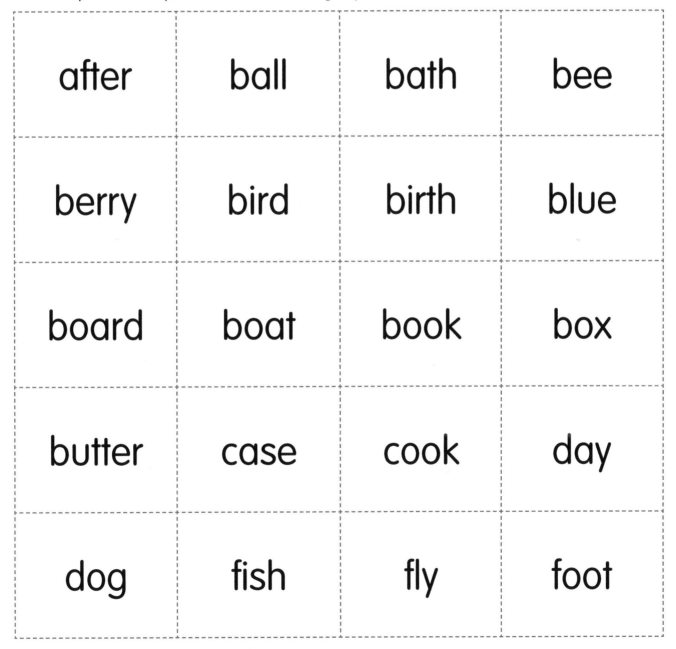

after	ball	bath	bee
berry	bird	birth	blue
board	boat	book	box
butter	case	cook	day
dog	fish	fly	foot

Compound Word Cards (cont.)

gold	guard	hand	hive
honey	house	in	life
line	milk	noon	note
out	paper	play	room
sand	scrap	shake	short
side	skate	step	story
straw	text	tub	work

10

What Is an Affix?

> An **affix** is a word part. It is a letter or group of letters added to the beginning or the end of a word that changes the meaning of the word. An affix is attached to a root or a base word to form a new word. Affixes can be prefixes or suffixes.

- When an affix is attached to the beginning of a word, the letter or group of letters added is called a *prefix*.

    re + act = react

- When an affix is attached to the end of a word, the added letter or group of letters is called a *suffix*.

    act + **s** = acts

    act + **ing** = acting

- Some words can have both prefixes and suffixes.

    un + comfort + **able** = uncomfortable

    re + mark + **able** = remarkable

    up + rise + **ing** = uprising

    un + **mis** + tak¢ + **able** = unmistakable

- Prefixes are not usually considered words when standing alone.

    dis-, **mis-**, **re-**, **sub-**, **un-**, **uni-**, **pre-**, **non-**, (exception: **a-**)

untied

- Suffixes are not usually considered words when standing alone.

    -s, **-ed**, **-ing**, **-tion**, **-ible**, **-al**, (exception: **-able**)

tied

- An affix added to a root word or base word gives a clue to the word's meaning.

    un + do = undo or to take apart; loosen

    art + **ist** = artist or one who does art

- Prefixes and suffixes can change the meaning of the word and/or the tense of the word.

    tie—**un**tie

    adjust—**re**adjust

    dance—danc**ed**, danc**er**

Common Prefixes List

Prefixes	Meaning	Examples
anti-	against	antisocial
ad-, at-	to, toward, add to	admit, attach
bi-	two	bicycle
con-, com-, co-	with, together, very	compact, contract, coworker
de-	undo, down, from	deduct
dis-, dif-, di-	not, in different directions	different, disable, divert
em-, en-	to put into, cause to	empower, enter
e-, ef-, ex-	out of	effect, emit, exit
ex-	out, pull out	extract, extricate, examine
im-, in-, il-	not	improper, invisible, illegal
im-, in-, il-	in, into, against	immigrate, inside, illustrate
micro-	tiny, very small	microscope
mis-	wrongly, wrong	misspell, misdeed
non-	without, not	nonfat
ob-	toward, up against	obstruct
post-	after, later	postgame, posttest
pre-	before	pregame, preschool, pretest
re-	again, back	redo, remake, retake, reject
sub-	under, below, down	submarine, subterranean, subtract
tri-	three	triangle, tricycle
trans-	across, beyond	transatlantic, transport
un-	not	unused, unhappy
under-	below, beneath	undercover, underneath, underwear

Play with Prefixes

Quick Lesson—When you add a prefix to a base word, it doesn't change the spelling of the base word. A prefix changes the meaning of the word it is added to, not the spelling.

Directions: Match the prefix in each ball to its definition in one of the bats. **Note:** More than one ball may go to the same bat. Also, a ball may go to more than one bat.

1.  dis

2.  mis

3.  pre

4.  un

5.  em

6.  re

7.  en

8.  im

9.  non

 opposite

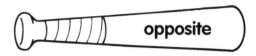 not

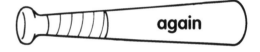 again

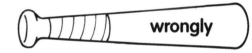 wrongly

 without

 before

 cause to

Prefixes: co-, com-, and con-

Directions: Combine each prefix and word to form a new word. Then, use two or more of the new words in one sentence.

1. co + captain = _____

2. co + operate = _____

3. co + pilot = _____

4. co + worker = _____

5. co + write = _____

Sentence: _____

_____

Directions: The words below begin with the suffixes **com-** or **con-**. Use each word in a sentence in order to show that you understand the meaning of the word. A dictionary may be used if needed.

6. company

_____

7. contact

_____

8. companion

_____

9. connect

_____

10. contract

_____

Prefix: de-

> **Quick Lesson**—The prefix *de-* means *down, out,* or *undo*.
>
> **Example:** de + throne = dethrone ➜ *Dethrone means removed from the throne.*
>
> **Sentence:** The people wanted to *dethrone* the king because he was not caring for them. They wanted him off of the throne and out of the kingdom.

Directions: Combine each *de-* prefix with the base word to create a new word. Write the meanings of the new words. Use a dictionary to help define words if necessary.

1. de + activate = _____

   _____

2. de + frost = _____

   _____

3. de + ice = _____

   _____

4. de + plane = _____

   _____

5. de + press = _____

   _____

Directions: Use one of the *de-* prefix words from above to fill in the sentences below.

6. My dad asked me to get the ice off the window. He wanted me to use the scraper to

   _____ the window.

7. The captain said it was time to get off the plane. We are going to _____ through the front door.

8. My mom is teaching my sister to drive. She told her to press down on the brake pedal to stop.

   She needed to _____ the brake pedal to stop.

9. There is so much frost in the freezer I can't get the ice cream out. I need to get the frost off of

   the ice cream. I need to _____ the freezer.

10. When we left for our trip, we had to activate the alarm. When we returned, we had to

    _____ the alarm so it wouldn't go off.

Bonus

Can you use the word *dehydrated* in a sentence? Use what you know about the prefix *de-* and a dictionary to help you with the word *hydrated*. Write the sentence on the back of the page.

Prefix: dis-

Directions: Use the clues to fill in the crossword puzzle. Every word begins with the prefix **dis-.**

Down

1. opposite of appear _____
2. opposite of order _____
3. opposite of agree _____
4. opposite of honest _____

Across

5. opposite of like _____
6. opposite of continue _____
7. opposite of obey _____

Name: _____

Prefixes

Prefixes: em- and en-

Quick Lesson—The prefixes **em-** and **en-** mean *give to* or *cause to*.

Sometimes, a word sounds better if the prefix has an **-m** ending and other times, the **-n** ending makes the word easier to pronounce.

Example: em + brace = embrace ➡ *Embrace* can mean *to hug* or *to like something*.

Sentence: My mom *embraces* my dad before a race. She gives him a hug.

or

Sue *embraced* the idea of learning how to swim so that she could take diving lessons.

Directions: Read the following sentences and decide which definition for **embrace** is correct. Put a check by your choice.

1. When I get home, I will embrace my sister!

   _____ **hug** _____ **to like something**

2. I like change. I embrace the idea of trying new things.

   _____ **hug** _____ **to like something**

Quick Lesson—The prefix **en-** means **cause to** or **give**. Sometimes, the **-n** ending makes the word easier to pronounce than the **-m** ending.

Example: En + gulf = engulf ➡ *En* means *cause to* and *gulf* can mean *surround*.

Sentence: The house was *engulfed* in flames. It was completely covered with fire when the fire trucks arrived.

Directions: Add the prefix **en-** to each of the base words or root words on the left in order to make a new word. Then draw a line from the new word to its definition.

3. _____able   cause to be better or richer

4. _____danger   help to do something

5. _____large   make bigger; cause to be bigger

6. _____rich   cause to get pleasure or happiness

7. _____tangle   put in danger; cause to be in danger

8. _____joy   tangle up; cause to be tangled

Bonus What do you think the word *empower* means? _____

Use the word *empower* in a sentence.

_____

_____

©Teacher Created Resources   17   *#3119 Building Words*

Prefixes: *im-* and *in-*

Quick Lesson—The prefixes *im-* and *in-* mean *not*.

Example: in + dependent = independent ➡ *Independent* means *not needing help* or *not dependent*.

Sentence: My big brother is *independent*. He has a job and takes care of himself.

Directions: Look at the *im-* and *in-* words and think about what each one means. Circle the best synonym or definition for each word.

1. **impolite**	rude	thoughtful
2. **impossible**	easy	very difficult
3. **inactive**	moving around	not doing anything
4. **incomplete**	not finished; partly done	finished; all done
5. **incorrect**	right; no mistakes	wrong; having errors
6. **inexpensive**	cheap	costing a lot
7. **invisible**	able to be seen	not able to be seen

Directions: Think about what each underlined word means and fill in the blanks in order to give examples.

8. It is <u>impolite</u> to _____.

9. It will be <u>impossible</u> to go swimming today. The pool is _____.

10. The worm was <u>inactive</u>. It was not _____.

11. My homework page is <u>incomplete</u>. I have _____.

12. The statement 2 + 2 = 5 is <u>incorrect</u>. It is not _____.

13. That shirt is <u>inexpensive</u>. It did not cost _____.

14. Air is <u>invisible</u>. You can't _____.

Prefix: mis-

Quick Lesson—The prefix **mis-** means **wrong**, **badly**, **wrongly**, or **incorrectly**.

Example: mis + dial = misdial ➡ To *misdial* means to dial incorrectly.

Sentence: I was in such a hurry that I *misdialed* my own phone number!

Directions: Draw a line from the word with the prefix **mis-** to its definition.

1. **mislead**   to be wrong, to choose incorrectly

2. **misspell**   to lead in the wrong direction

3. **mistake**   to put something in the wrong place

4. **misunderstand**   to spell incorrectly

5. **misuse**   to understand incorrectly

6. **misplace**   to use incorrectly

Directions: Use the words above with the prefix **mis-** to fill in the sentences below.

7. He tried to _____ me about how hard the hike would be.
   He said it was easy.

8. I did not want to _____ my jacket during practice so I put it
   in my bag.

9. Be careful not to _____ any of the words in your writing
   assignment. Spelling counts!

10. I _____ the assignments unless I pay attention to everything
    the teacher says.

11. If you _____ the bike pump, the tire might explode!

12. Did you _____ me for my identical twin brother? Don't
    worry, it happens all the time!

Bonus

Think about what you have learned about the prefix **mis-**. Explain what the following
word would mean and use it in a sentence.

Mistreat means _____

Sentence: _____

_____

Prefixes: non- and un-

> **Quick Lesson**—The prefix **non-** means **not** or **the opposite.**
>
> **Example:** non + fiction = nonfiction ➜ *Nonfiction* means *not fiction.*
>
> **Sentence:** If a book is *nonfiction,* the facts or the story is true.

Directions: Write the meaning of each of these **non-** words. Use what you know about the prefix **non-** and a dictionary to help you.

1. nonliving _____

2. nonstick _____

3. nondairy _____

4. nonhuman _____

5. nonfat _____

> **Quick Lesson**—The prefix **un-** means **not** or **the opposite.**
>
> **Example:** un + known = unknown or not known.
>
> **Sentence:** The author of the book is *unknown.* The author is not known.

Directions: Form new words that mean the same as each phrase by adding **un-** to the base word. Write the new word and circle the prefix. On the lines provided, write a sentence using each new word.

6. not fair = _____

_____

7. not happy = _____

_____

8. not broken = _____

_____

9. not known = _____

_____

10. not locked = _____

_____

Prefixes: pre- and post-

Quick Lesson—The prefix *pre-* means *before*.

Example: pre + soak = presoak → *Presoak* means *to soak before.*

Sentence: My dad *presoaks* his socks before he washes them.

Directions: Choose the correct word from the word bank for each sentence.

Word Bank	preschool	preboard	predict	preorder	prevent

1. Children get to _____ airplanes before other passengers.

2. We will _____ our school pictures today, and the order will be ready next month.

3. The weatherman is going to _____ rain again!

4. My brother went to _____ last year, but he is in kindergarten now.

5. Be careful with campfires to _____ forest fires.

Quick Lesson—The prefix *post-* means *after*.

Example: post + date = postdate → *Postdate* means to put a date that is later than the current date.

Sentence: We will *postdate* the check in order to make a later payment.

Directions: Choose the correct word to complete each sentence and circle it. Cross out the other option. Pay attention to the two prefixes, *pre-* which means *before* and *post-* which means *after*.

6. We are ordering a pizza postgame. We will eat | before after | the game.

7. A posttest is taken | before after | the test.

8. A pretest is taken | before after | the test.

9. You should preheat an oven | before after | baking a cake.

10. We got to preview the movie and see it | before after | the other class.

Prefix: re-

> **Quick Lesson**—The prefix **re-** means **again**, **back**, or **once more**.
>
> **Example:** re + heat = reheat ➜ *Reheat* means to *heat something again*.
>
> **Sentence:** We are going to *reheat* the soup we made. Mom says we shouldn't eat cold soup.

Directions: Add the prefix **re-** to each word and draw a line to its definition.

1. re + build = _____   to make smaller

2. re + cycle = _____   to process old items to make new items

3. re + duce = _____   to say you will not do something

4. re + search = _____   to use something again

5. re + fuse = _____   to find out more about something

6. re + use = _____   to build or create something again

7. re + write = _____   to write something again

Directions: Use the words in the links to fill in the blank in each sentence.

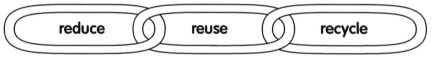

reduce   **reuse**   **recycle**

8. We are trying to _____ the amount of garbage at home. Our goal is to have less garbage each week.

9. We _____ by sorting our bottles and cans. Then we take them to the Recycling Center.

10. We use cloth bags at the grocery store. We can _____ the same bags again and again.

Bonus What could you make with a soup can if you wanted to reuse it instead of throwing it away? Draw a picture. You may use one of the can outlines or the empty space.

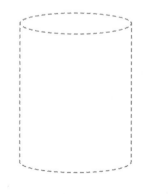

Prefix: *tele-*

Quick Lesson—The prefix *tele-* can mean *a far distance* or *distant*. (*Tele* is also a root.)

Example: tele + commute = telecommute ➜ *Telecommute* means *to work from a distance using a computer connection to an office.*

Sentence: My mom gets to *telecommute* three days a week instead of driving to her office.

Directions: Look at the picture dictionary entries. Match the word with the **tele-** prefix to its entry.

1.
   telegram

2.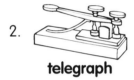
   telegraph

3.
   telephone

4.
   telephoto lens

5.
   telescope

6.
   television

- an instrument used to view objects far away

- a message sent from far away by a telegraph

- an old way to send messages from far away using wires

- a device that sends voices over long distances

- a large lens to take pictures of things far away

- an electronic system to transmit pictures and sound

Bonus

What do you think a *telemarketer* does? _____
_____

Look up *telemarketer* in the dictionary and write the definition below. _____
_____

Did you have the right idea?   **Yes**   **No**

The Prefix Comes First

Quick Lesson—Prefixes are the letters that come before a word. When you add a prefix to the beginning of a word, you change its meaning.

Example: re + do = redo ➔ *Redo* means to *do again*.

Sentence: I need to *redo* my homework because it is too messy!

Directions: Add the correct prefix to the beginning of each word in order to match the definition. Use your Common Prefixes List (page 12) if you need help. Each prefix can be used more than once.

Prefixes	pre-	re-	un-	mis-

1. _____ use = use incorrectly

2. _____ order = order before

3. _____ organize = set up differently; rearrange

4. _____ place = put back

5. _____ understand = understand incorrectly

6. _____ tell = tell again

7. _____ usual = not ordinary

8. _____ lock = open

9. _____ do = unfasten or release

10. _____ school = school before elementary school

Bonus Cross out the words with prefixes that do not make sense.

delock   misuse   undo   mistake

reorder   unwake   preschool   deschool

Add a Prefix, Make an Opposite

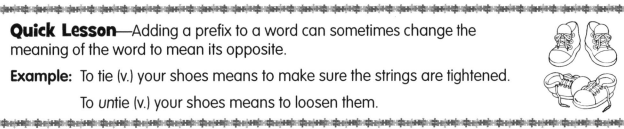

Quick Lesson—Adding a prefix to a word can sometimes change the meaning of the word to mean its opposite.

Example: To tie (v.) your shoes means to make sure the strings are tightened.

To *untie* (v.) your shoes means to loosen them.

Directions: Look at the **boldface** words and definitions below and underline the prefixes. Write a new definition for each opposite meaning. Use the Common Prefixes List (page 12) and a dictionary.

1. **fiction** (n.) – stories that describe imaginary characters and events

   nonfiction (n.) – _____

2. **happy** (adj.) – show pleasure

   unhappy (adj.) – _____

3. **active** (adj.) – working and full of energy

   inactive (adj.) – _____

4. **caring** (adj.) – having concern for someone or something

   uncaring (adj.) – _____

5. **internal** (adj.) – from the inside

   external (adj.) – _____

6. **appear** (v.) – be visible or noticeable

   disappear (v.) – _____

7. **enable** (v.) – allow something to happen or someone to do something

   disable (v.) – _____

8. **cover** (v.) – to put something on top of or over to block it from view

   uncover (v.) – _____

Bonus   **overestimate** (v.) to place too much value on something

   underestimate (v.) _____

Which word would you use to fill in the sentence below?

Sometimes I _____ how much time it will take to do my homework.

Change the Prefix, Change the Meaning

Quick Lesson—If you change the prefix of a base word, you will change its meaning. This change can be small, or it can make the word mean something completely different.

Example: The adjective *usual* can mean regular or "everyday." When you add the prefix **un-** to the word *usual*, you get *unusual*, which can mean different, irregular, or out of the ordinary. *Usual* and *unusual* are opposites.

Directions: A word and its definition are provided on the first line. On the second line, a prefix has been added to the word. Use your Common Prefixes List (page 12) and a dictionary to find definitions. Write the definitions for the new words on the lines provided.

1. **worker** (n.) – someone who performs a job or task

    coworker (n.) – _____

2. **make** (v.) – to create something

    remake (v.) – _____

3. **ordinary** (adj.) – common or usual

    extraordinary (adj.) – _____

4. **place** (v.) – to put something in a certain location

    misplace (v.) – _____

5. **unite** (v.) – to come together; join

    reunite (v.) – _____

6. **pretest** (n.) – a practice test that is given before the actual test

    posttest (n.) – _____

7. **megaphone** (n.) – a funnel-shaped device used to make a voice sound louder

    telephone (n.) – _____

8. **conduct** (n.) – the way a person behaves

    misconduct (n.) – _____

Bonus Define the words that were created by adding different prefixes to the word *cover*.

cover (v.) – to put something over, on top of, or in front of

9. **discover** (v.) – _____

10. **recover** (v.) – _____

11. **uncover** (v.) – _____

Same Prefixes, Different Base Words

Quick Lesson—The same prefix can be added to many different base words to form new words.

Examples: The prefix *under-* can make the words *understand*, *underway*, *undergo*, *underwear*, and *underneath*.

Directions: Write the meaning of each prefix in the center of each triangle. Use your Common Prefixes List (page 12) to help you. In the frame, write a word on each side of the triangle that uses the prefix. *Hint:* Turn your paper to help you write.

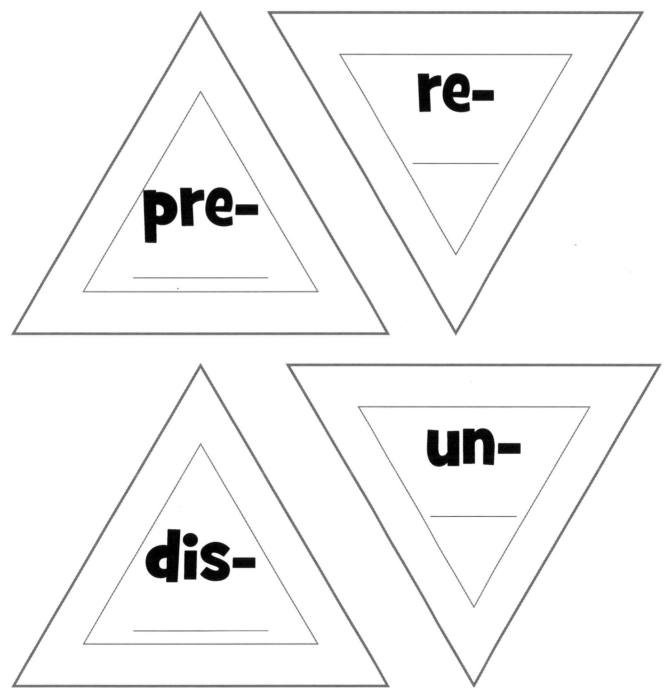

Prefixes Review

Directions: Match a prefix to a base word. Use the new word in a sentence and circle the new word. Each prefix or base word may be used more than once.

Prefixes		Base Words			
dis-	re-	able	draw	new	school
pre-	un-	agree	equal	please	view

1. _____

_____

2. _____

_____

3. _____

_____

4. _____

_____

5. _____

_____

6. _____

_____

Directions: Fill in the blanks to define each word with a prefix.

7. If <u>important</u> means having value or being special, then <u>unimportant</u> means _____

_____.

8. If <u>usual</u> means ordinary, then <u>unusual</u> means _____

_____.

9. If <u>polite</u> means being respectful, then <u>impolite</u> means _____

_____.

10. If something is <u>possible</u>, it can be done. If something is <u>impossible</u>, it _____

_____.

Numerical Prefixes List

Quick Lesson—Some prefixes modify words by telling how many. The chart below shows the most popular numerical prefixes we use in the English language:

How many?	Prefix	Examples
1	uni-	unicorn unicycle uniform
	mono-	monocle monorail
2	bi-	bicycle binoculars biplane
3	tri-	triangle tricycle triathlete triplets triceratops tripod
4	quadr-	quadrant quadrilateral quadruplets
	quar-	quarter quartet
5	penta-	pentagon
	quint-	quintuplets
6	hexa-	hexagon
8	oct-	octagon October* octave octopus * Long ago, October was the 8th month, not the 10th month, as it is now.
10	dec-	decade decimal decathlon
100	cent-	centimeter centipede century
1,000	milli-	millennium millimeter millipede
	kilo-	kilogram kilometer kilowatt

How Many?

> **Quick Lesson**—A numerical prefix is one that has to do with numbers. The prefix tells you how many.

Directions: Fill in the missing words by referring to the Numerical Prefixes List (page 29). Circle the word or words in each sentence that gave you a clue.

1. A dinosaur with three horns on its head is called a _____.

2. A shape with eight sides is called a _____.

3. Another word for one hundred years is a _____.

4. A _____ is a magical horse with one horn on its head.

5. A thousand years is called a _____.

6. An ocean animal with eight legs is called an _____.

7. There are ten years in a _____.

8. _____ are a pair of lenses used to help you view objects far away.

9. Elsa and her two sisters were all born on the same day. The three sisters are called

   _____.

10. I just got a new _____ with two wheels and a basket.

Directions: Write the number of sides each shape has inside the shape. Write the name of each shape on the line underneath it. Use the Numerical Prefixes List (page 29) to help you.

_____   _____   _____   _____

Name: _____

How Many Musicians?

Quick Lesson—A numerical prefix is one that has to do with numbers. The prefix tells you **how many**.

Directions: Count the musicians in each picture to fill in the first blank.

To fill in the second blank, think about the prefixes you already know. Use a dictionary and the Word Bank to help you correctly label each group.

Word Bank	duo	quartet	quintet	sextet	trio

1. Here is a group with _____ musicians.

   It is called a _____.

2. Here is a group with _____ musicians.

   It is called a _____.

3. Here is a group with _____ musicians.

   It is called a _____.

4. Here is a group with _____ musicians.

   It is called a _____.

5. Here is a group with _____ musicians.

   It is called a _____.

Bonus

When two singers sing a song together, it is called a _____.

duet   trio   quartet   sextet

Numerical Prefixes Review

Directions: Use a word with a numerical prefix to label the picture in each box. Use your Numerical Prefixes List (page 29) if necessary.

1. _____	2. _____	3. _____
4. _____	5. _____	6. _____
7. _____	8. _____	9. _____
10. _____	11. _____	12. _____

Common Suffixes List

Suffixes	Meaning	Examples
-able, -ible	able to be	likeable, flexible
-ation, -tion	something that	formation, creation
-cian	someone who	electrician
-d, -ed	done in the past	skated, washed
-en, -n	a completed action, to make	eaten, moisten, golden
-er	more	kinder
-es, -s	more than one	pits, peaches
-est	most	kindest
-ful	full of	helpful
-ing	currently doing	writing
-ist	someone who	artist
-less	without	hopeless
-ly	how something is done	slowly
-ment	state of being	contentment
-ness	state of being	happiness
-or, -er, -ar	someone who	actor, teacher, scholar
-sion	something that	explosion
-y	described by	rainy

Identify the Suffixes

Quick Lesson—You hear and use suffixes everyday. Suffixes change a word's meaning. Knowing the meanings of different suffixes will help you decode new words.

Example: If you add an **-s** to *tree*, you get *trees*.

You change tree, meaning one tree, to trees, meaning more than one tree.

Directions: Look at the common suffixes below and use your Common Suffixes List (page 33) to find their meanings. Give an example for each new suffix.

	Suffixes	Definition	Example
1.	-s or -es		
2.	-less		
3.	-ful		
4.	-able; -ible		
5.	-est		
6.	-ation and -tion		
7.	-ing		
8.	-d and -ed		
9.	-en and -n		
10.	–or, -er, and -ar		
11.	-cian		
12.	-ness		

Play with Suffixes

Quick Lesson— Suffixes are word parts. They are not usually words by themselves. When a suffix is attached to a word, the word's meaning changes.

Directions: Match the suffix in each ball to its definition in one of the bats. Use the Common Suffixes List (page 33) to find their meanings. **Note:** More than one ball may go to the same bat.

1. -cian

2. -ing

3. -less

4. -tion -sion

5. -ly

6. -ness

7. -or -er -ar

8. -n, -en

9. -able

10. -ment

able to be

currently doing

without

how something is done

state of being

someone who

show a completed action

something that

Suffixes: -ar, -er, and -or

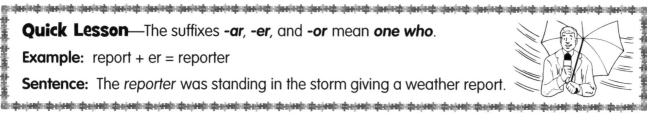

Quick Lesson—The suffixes *-ar*, *-er*, and *-or* mean **one who**.

Example: report + er = reporter

Sentence: The *reporter* was standing in the storm giving a weather report.

Directions: Circle the correct ending for each verb and create a noun. Use the new noun you created in a sentence. If needed, use a dictionary.

1. **teach**   or   er   ar   (n.) _____

   _____

2. **act**   or   er   ar   (n.) _____

   _____

3. **sing**   or   er   ar   (n.) _____

   _____

4. **collect**   or   er   ar   (n.) _____

   _____

5. **sculpt**   or   er   ar   (n.) _____

   _____

6. **dance**   or   er   ar   (n.) _____

   _____

7. **print**   or   er   ar   (n.) _____

   _____

8. **direct**   or   er   ar   (n.) _____

   _____

9. **beg**   or   er   ar   (n.) _____

   _____

10. **instruct** or   er   ar   (n.) _____

   _____

Bonus

What do you think the word **scholar** means? Use a dictionary if you need help with the definition.

_____

_____

Suffixes: -d and -ed

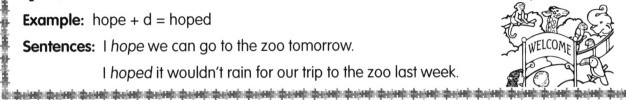

Quick Lesson—The suffixes **-d** and **-ed** mean that an action has been completed.

Example: hope + d = hoped

Sentences: I *hope* we can go to the zoo tomorrow.

I *hoped* it wouldn't rain for our trip to the zoo last week.

Adding the suffixes **-d** and **-ed** to regular verbs changes them to past tense. The rules in the chart will help you decide which suffix to add:

If the word ends with a . . .	Do this . . .	Examples
consonant + vowel + consonant	double the final consonant before adding "-ed"	stop → stopped
consonant + "e"	just add "d"	bake → baked
"-ie"	just add "d"	die → died
double consonant	just add "-ed"	pick → picked
consonant + "y"	change the "y" to an "i" and add "-ed"	try → tried
vowel + "y"	just add "-ed"	play → played

Directions: Look at the words below. Write the past tense form of the verb in the oval on the right side. Follow the rules above for adding the correct suffixes to each word.

1. decay

2. doze

3. grin

4. absorb

5. pause

6. starve

7. supply

8. untie

Suffixes: -en and -n

Quick Lesson—The suffixes **-en** and **-n** can be added to a verb to make it show a completed action.

Examples: He has *eaten* all of the dessert. All of the dessert has been *eaten*.
He has caused all of the dessert to be *eaten*.

Directions: Change each word below by adding the suffixes **-n** or **-en** to make the word show a completed action.

1. **awake** + _____ = _____

2. **broke** + _____ = _____

3. **stole** + _____ = _____

4. **take** + _____ = _____

5. **length** + _____ = _____

6. **moist** + _____ = _____

7. **sharp** + _____ = _____

8. **short** + _____ = _____

9. **white** + _____ = _____

10. **sweet** + _____ = _____

Quick Lesson—The suffix **-en** can change a noun to an adjective to suggest *made of*.

Example: silk + en = silken ➔ **Sentence:** The *silken* robe was beautiful.

Directions: Add **-en** to each noun to change it to an adjective and use it to describe something.

11. **gold** + _____ = _____

12. **wood** + _____ = _____

13. **wool** + _____ = _____

Quick Lesson—The suffix -en can change an adjective or a noun to a verb.

Example: tight + en = tighten ➔ **Sentence:** I will *tighten* the knot on my shoelace.

Directions: Add **-en** or **-n** to the words below to change them to verbs. Use each in a sentence.

14. **strength** + _____ = _____

_____

15. **loose** + _____ = _____

_____

38

Suffix: -ful

> **Quick Lesson**—The suffix *-ful* means **full of**. Even though the suffix means *full of*, there is only one *l* at the end.
>
> **Example:** truth + *ful* = truthful or full of truth   **Sentence:** The answer was *truthful*, not false.

Directions: Read the whole story and review the **-ful** words in the doghouse Word Bank below. Use those words to fill in the blanks and complete the story.

A Wonderful Surprise

When Charlie looked out the window he saw a _____ rainbow.
1

Then he heard a sound. Maybe this was going to be his lucky day. He crossed his fingers.

He was _____ the new puppy would arrive today.
2

He ran outside to see his mom sitting on the grass, holding an _____
3

of laundry. Or was it laundry? The next thing he knew, the towels she was holding moved,

and out popped a very _____ little puppy. It jumped and rolled
4

on the grass.

Charlie's mom said, "Be _____. The puppy needs to get
5

comfortable around us."

Later, Charlie, who was always _____, gave the puppy a
6

_____ of food. The puppy ate a _____
7   8

and then went back to playing.

It was a _____ scene.
9

WORD BANK

armful	helpful	mouthful
careful	hopeful	playful
colorful	joyful	scoopful

Suffix: -ing

Quick Lesson—The suffix **-ing** can mean *something is happening now* or an *action that is continuing*.

Example: work + *ing* = working ➜ **Sentence:** Right now, I am *working* on a project for school.

Directions: Read the sentences and choose the correct **-ing** word to complete each one.

Word Bank	playing	running	smelling
	thinking	touching	waiting

1. I am _____ basketball with my brother.

2. He is _____ the lizard in the tank.

3. She's _____ the flowers in the vase.

4. I am _____ as fast as I can.

5. Are you _____ for a ride home?

6. What are you _____ about?

Quick Lesson—When adding **-ing** to words ending in the silent **e**, drop the **e** and add **-ing**.

Example: snore – e + *ing* = snoring. ➜ **Sentence:** My uncle was *snoring* loudly.

Directions: Change the following words by adding **-ing**.

7. **Taste** – _____ + _____ = _____

8. **Locate** – _____ + _____ = _____

Quick Lesson—When adding **-ing** to words ending in **ie**, change the **ie** to **y** and add **-ing**.

Example: die – (ie) + y + *ing* = dying. ➜ The plant is *dying* because it needs water.

Directions: Change the following words by adding **-ing**.

9. **untie** – _____ + _____ + _____ = _____

10. **lie** – _____ + _____ + _____ = _____

Suffix: -less

> **Quick Lesson**—The suffix **-less** can mean **without** or **missing**. When you add **-less** to a noun, it changes the noun to an adjective. Often, the new word means the opposite.
>
> **Example:** care + *less* = careless ➔ *careless* means without a care; not being careful
>
> **Sentence:** The people were *careless* and left their trash in the park after the party.
>
> **Reminder:** When the adjective ends with **y**, simply change the **y** to an **i** and add your suffix. To add the suffix **-less** to the word penny, drop the **y** and add an **i**.
>
> **Example:** penny + *less* = penny – y + i + *less* = penniless ➔ *penniless* means having no money

Directions: Complete the chart below. Read the word in column A and then write the base word next to it in column B. Add the suffix in column C, and write the definition for each word in column D. Use a dictionary if you need help. The first one is done for you.

-less = without; missing			
A Word	**B** Base Word	**C** Suffix	**D** Definition
1. harmless	harm	less	without harm; not causing harm
2. fearless			
3. thoughtless			
4. speechless			
5. thankless			
6. worthless			
7. useless			
8. hopeless			

Directions: Add the suffix **-less** to the word that is under the line in each sentence.

9. A superhero has no fear. He is _____ .
fear

10. She was so surprised she couldn't talk. She was _____ .
speech

11. An ostrich cannot fly. It is a _____ bird.
flight

12. Our new baby is _____ . She needs our help for everything!
help

Suffix: -ly

Quick Lesson—Adding the suffix **-ly** to an adjective creates a word that *describes how something is done*.

    Example: kind + ly = kindly ➔ The adjective *kind* becomes *kindly*, an adverb.

    Sentences: The *kind* man helped the little boy build the birdhouse.

                   The man *kindly* helped the little boy with his project.

★ When the adjective ends with **y**, simply change the **y** to an **i** and add your suffix.

    Example: happy + ly = happily

    Sentences: The *happy* children played at the party.

                 The children played *happily* at the party.

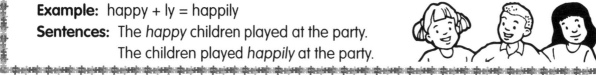

Directions: Change each adjective to an adverb and write its definition or a synonym.

1. anxious + ly = _____

   _____

2. generous + ly = _____

   _____

3. cautious + ly = _____

   _____

4. mysterious + ly = _____

   _____

5. grumpy + ly = _____

   _____

Directions: Add **-ly** to the adjectives below to create adverbs. Use each adverb in a sentence to describe how something is done.

6. slow + ly = _____

   _____

7. easy + ly = _____

   _____

8. curious + ly = _____

   _____

9. angry + ly = _____

   _____

Bonus   Write three adverbs that describe how you do your homework.

_____   _____   _____

Suffix: -ment

Quick Lesson—The suffix **-ment** means *act of or state of being*.

Example: content + ment = contentment ➜ *Contentment* means being content or being satisfied.

Sentence: There was a feeling of *contentment* in the room once the project was finished.

Directions: Add the suffix **-ment** to each word and write the new word. Use each word to complete one of the sentences in the next section.

1. amaze + _____ = _____

2. enjoy + _____ = _____

3. move + _____ = _____

4. improve + _____ = _____

5. enlarge + _____ = _____

6. treat + _____ = _____

Directions: Use one of the words with the suffix **-ment** from above to complete the sentences below.

7. My dad made an _____ of my school picture to send to my grandma.

8. The new paint was quite an _____ for the old house. It looked much better.

9. We have a new _____ class at school in which we get to dance and move around.

10. When she opened her present she had a look of _____. She was so surprised.

11. There is a new _____ for my allergy. It helps me breathe better.

12. My grandpa gets _____ from working in his garden. It makes him happy.

Suffix: -ness

Quick Lesson—The suffix **-ness** means **being** or **the state of being**.

Example: soft + ness = softness ➜ *Softness* means being soft.

Sentence: The *softness* of the blanket made her want to cuddle up in it.

Directions: Draw a line to match the words ending in the **-ness** suffix that are antonyms.

1. dryness   happiness

2. sadness   hopefulness

3. fullness   emptiness

4. hopelessness   wetness

Quick Lesson—When a base word ends in **y**, change the **y** to **i** and add the suffix **-ness**.

Example: stuffy (– y) + i + *ness* = stuffiness ➜ *Stuffiness* means being *stuffy*.

Sentence: The *stuffiness* of the room made the students sleepy.

Directions: Change each adjective to a noun by adding **-ness**. Don't forget the **y** rule if you need it.

5. silly _____

6. goofy _____

7. kind _____

8. friendly _____

9. happy _____

10. fair _____

11. sweet _____

12. cheerful _____

13. grumpy _____

14. ugly _____

Change the y to an i.

Bonus

What do you think the word *business* means? _____

_____

Suffixes: -sion and -tion

> **Quick Lesson**—The suffix **-sion** can mean **something that**.
> Base words often change when adding **-sion**.
>
> **Example:** explode + sion = explosion
>
> **Note:** The **-de** ending was dropped to add the suffix.
>
> **Sentence:** When the mountain exploded, the *explosion* was heard in the next town!

Directions: Look at the base word and the suffix and think about what word the combination could make. Change the base word and write what each combination becomes. Explain what changed. Use a dictionary if you need help.

1. The word **decide** + *sion* becomes _____.

2. The word **conclude** + *sion* becomes _____.

3. The word **revise** + *sion* becomes _____.

4. The word **discuss** + *sion* becomes _____.

5. The word **admit** + *sion* becomes _____.

> **Quick Lesson**—The suffix **-tion** can also mean **something that**.
>
> **Example:** attract + *tion* = attraction   ➜   An *attraction* is something that attracts.
>
> **Sentence:** The new baby gorilla is the main *attraction* at the nature center.
>
> **Note:** Only one **t** is used at the end to add the suffix.

Directions: Add the suffix **-tion** to each of the words below.

6. connect + *tion* = _____

7. direct + *tion* = _____

8. elect + *tion* = _____

> **Quick Lesson**—When adding **-tion** to a word ending in an **e**, drop the **e** first.
>
> **Example:** create + *tion* = creation   ➜   A *creation* is something that is created.
>
> **Sentence:** His birthday cake was an amazing *creation*. It looked like a real car.

Directions: Add the suffix **-tion** to each of the words below.

9. educate + *tion* = _____

10. illustrate + *tion* = _____

11. imitate + *tion* = _____

Changing Parts of Speech

Quick Lesson—You can change the part of speech of a word when you add or change the suffix. Sometimes the meaning will change, too.

Examples: ➜ My *fish* is cool. (*noun*—person, place, thing)

➜ I like to go *fishing*. (*verb*—action or state of being)

➜ My lunchbox has a *fishy* smell. (*adjective*—a word that describes a noun)

Directions: Write the parts of speech (adjective, noun, or verb) of each of the bolded words in the blanks below. Notice how suffixes change each word. The first one has been done for you.

1. **salt** __noun_____

   The potatoes taste **salty**. __adjective_____

   He always **salts** his food before he tastes it. __verb_____

2. **friend** _____

   You are my **friends**. _____

   You are **friendly**. _____

3. **love** _____

   I **loved** my grandma. _____

   That is a **lovely** dress you are wearing. _____

4. **like** _____

   Dogs are **likable**. _____

   My brother's **likely** choice will be the cookie, not the carrot. _____

5. **bake** _____

   Do you sell **baked** goods? _____

   I love **baking** cakes. _____

Bonus

Add suffixes to the base word "water" to make a noun, a verb, and an adjective. Then, use each new word in a sentence.

6. **Noun:** water + _____ = _____

7. **Verb:** water + _____ = _____

8. **Adjective:** water + _____ = _____

Suffixes and the Silent "e"

Quick Lesson—A silent "e" at the end of a base word doesn't make a sound. If you notice a silent "e" at the end of a word when adding a suffix, think about the different rules.

Keep the silent "e" if the suffix starts with a consonant.

Example: arrange + *ment* = arrangement   pride + *ful* = prideful

Directions: Change each word by adding a suffix.

1. use + *less* = _____

2. live + *ly* = _____

3. shame + *less* = _____

4. taste + *less* = _____

5. hope + *ful* = _____

6. waste + *ful* = _____

7. peace + *ful* = _____

8. fortunate + *ly* = _____

-less

-ly

-ful

Quick Lesson—Drop the silent "e" before adding a suffix that begins with a vowel sound.

Example: spic~~e~~ + y = spicy   (Cross out the silent e.)

Directions: Change each word by adding a suffix. Remember to cross out the silent **e** before you add the suffix that starts with a vowel, even if the vowel is another **e**! The first one has been done.

9. past~~e~~ + *ed* = _____ pasted _____

10. mistake + *en* = _____

11. drive + *er* = _____

12. loose + *er* = _____

13. wise + *est* = _____

14. grade + *ing* = _____

15. write + *ing* = _____

16. close + *est* = _____

-est

-ed

-er

-ing

Suffixes Review

Directions: Use the suffixes at the top of the chart to make some new words using the base words that are on the left side. If a word ends in **y**, you may need to change a letter.

Note: There will be some blanks in each column when a suffix does not work with a base word.

Suffix	-ed	-er	-ful	-less	-ly
call					
dance					
happy					
help					
hope					
smile					

Directions: A suffix can change the tense of a word from *past*, to *present, or future*. Write the tense of each of the bolded verbs in the sentences below.

Examples: I **cooked** dinner yesterday. (past tense)

I am **cooking** right now. (present tense)

I will **cook** for you tomorrow. (future tense)

1. Are you **making** a card now? _____

2. He is **reading** his favorite book. _____

3. She will **rest** when her chores are done. _____

4. I **jogged** on the track yesterday. _____

5. I am **walking** to the store. _____

6. I **made** you a present. _____

7. I **used** oil to fry the eggs for breakfast. _____

8. Yesterday, I **walked** all around the zoo. _____

Directions: Cross out the word that is **not** spelled correctly in each box.

9	happyness	happiness	12	peacefull	peaceful
10	running	runing	13	direction	directtion
11	disslike	dislike	14	easyly	easily

Plural Suffixes: Adding -es to y Endings

Quick Lesson—To make a word that ends with a **y** plural, change the **y** to **i** and add **es**.

Example: blueberry   ➔ drop the **y** and add **i + es** = blueberries

Directions: Read each sentence and circle the singular word that should be a plural word. Write the plural word on the line next to the sentence.

1. Did you see all the fairy in the kindergarten parade? _____

2. Do you like cherry on your ice cream? _____

3. All the baby in the nursery were crying at the same time. _____

4. Our dog had five puppy last night! _____

5. My big brother works hard on his study. _____

6. I like to eat blueberries and blackberry in the summer. _____

Directions: Write the singular word for each plural word.

7. strawberries _____

8. cities _____

9. pennies _____

Directions: Write the correct plural word for each picture

10. _____   11. _____   12. _____

Plural Suffixes: Adding -s and -es to o Endings

Quick Lesson—If a word ends in a **vowel** plus an **o**, just add an **-s** to the end of the word to make it a plural.

Example: video + *s* = videos

Directions: Add an **-s** to each noun below to make it a plural noun.

1. patio _____   3. igloo _____

2. stereo _____   4. radio _____

Quick Lesson—If a word ends in a consonant plus an **o**, add **-es** to the end of the word to make it a plural.

Example: mosquito + *es* = mosquitoes

Directions: Add an **-es** to each noun below to make it a plural noun.

5. buffalo _____   7. tomato _____

6. potato _____   8. volcano _____

Quick Lesson—Some words ending in the letter "**o**" do not seem to follow any rules. The best way to learn the plural forms of these words is to memorize them.

Directions: Use a dictionary to find the plural form of each word that is in the Word Bank. Place the word in the proper column and then add the correct ending. The first one has been done for you.

Word Bank	Add -s	Add -es
auto	autos	
echo		
hero		
memo		
studio		
veto		
zero		
zoo		

Plural Suffixes: Adding -es Endings

Quick Lesson—When a noun ends in **c, ch, s, sh, x**, or **z**, add **-es** to the end of the word.

Example: wish + *es* = wishes   buzz + *es* = buzzes

Directions: Label each picture below with the correct plural word for each noun.

1. _____

2. _____

3. _____

4. _____

5. _____

Quick Lesson—When a noun ends in an **f** or an **fe**, the **f** is often changed to a **v** before adding **-es** to the end of the word.

Example: *knife* would change to *knives*

Directions: Write the correct plural form for each noun.

6. scarf _____   9. leaf _____

7. elf _____   10. life _____

8. wolf _____   11. shelf _____

Quick Lesson—Some words that end in **f** or **fe** do not change and an **s** is added directly to these endings. The easiest way to learn them is to memorize them.

Directions: Add an **-s** to the following words to make them plural.

12. staff _____   14. chef _____

13. safe _____   15. reef _____

Plural Nouns Review

Directions: Write the plural form of each noun by adding the correct plural suffix.

1. wish _____
2. diary _____
3. calf _____
4. potato _____
5. house _____
6. rodeo _____
7. story _____
8. fable _____
9. ranch _____

10. shelf _____
11. piano _____
12. bus _____
13. country _____
14. volcano _____
15. day _____
16. sprout _____
17. video _____
18. loaf _____

Quick Lesson—Many plural nouns do not follow any of the rules that the words above follow. These are called rule breakers, or irregular plural nouns. Instead of adding a suffix, the spelling of the entire word changes.

Example: person → people

Directions: Label each picture. Draw a line from each singular noun to its irregular plural form.

19. _____   _____

20. _____   _____

21. _____   _____

22. _____   _____

23. _____   _____

24. _____   _____

Suffixes: -er and -r

Quick Lessons—The suffix **-er** is added to an adjective in order to compare two things. When the adjective ends in an **e**, just add the **-r**.

When the adjective ends with **y**, simply change the **y** to an **i** and add your suffix.

Examples and Sentences:

sweet + er = sweeter   ➜   The iced tea tastes *sweeter* with sugar added.

nice + r = nicer   ➜   Our car looks *nicer* when it is clean.

pretty + i +er = prettier   ➜   I think the dress with the long sleeves is *prettier*.

Directions: Look at the pictures in each row. Write a sentence comparing the two pictures. Use a word in your sentence that has an **-er** suffix in order to show the comparison.

1. _____

_____

2. _____

_____

3. _____

_____

Bonus

Look at each pair of pictures above. Think of another way to compare one set of pictures. Write the new sentences below. Don't forget to use a word in your sentence that has an **-er** suffix to show the comparison.

_____

_____

_____

_____

Suffixes: -est and -st

> **Quick Lesson**—The suffix **-est** is added to an adjective in order to compare more than two things.
>
> **Example:** tall + est = tallest
>
> **Sentence:** Julie is the *tallest* student in my school.
>
> **Example:** late + st = latest ➜ When the adjective ends in an **e**, just add the **-st**.
>
> **Sentence:** The *latest* we can stay outside is 7 p.m.

Directions: Look at the following words used to compare. Add the adjective to each line that compares *more* than two things.

1. large   larger   _____

2. green   greener   _____

3. cold   colder   _____

4. wise   wiser   _____

> **Quick Lesson**—When a word ends in a **y**, change the **y** to an **i** and then add **-est**.
>
> **Example:** lazy + i + *est* = laziest
>
> **Sentence:** Our cat is the *laziest* cat. He never chases anything!

Directions: Look at the following words used to compare. First add the adjective to compare two things, then add the adjective that compares more than two things. Don't forget the **y** rule. The first one has been done for you.

5. **spicy** _____spicier_____   _____spiciest_____

6. **salty** _____   _____

7. **friendly** _____   _____

> **Quick Lesson**—When a word ends in a vowel + a consonant, double the consonant and add **-est**.
>
> **Example:** big + est = biggest

Directions: Write the adjectives used to compare two things and more than two things next to each adjective below. Don't forget the "double the consonant" rule.

8. **flat** _____   _____

9. **sad** _____   _____

10. **slim** _____   _____

Suffixes for Comparing Review

Directions: Fill in the chart below using suffixes to compare.

Adjective	Comparing Two Items	Comparing More Than Two Items
1. frail		
2. harsh		
3. scary		
4. simple		
5. brief		
6. risky		
7. swift		
8. easy		
9. chilly		
10. hard		
11. slimy		
12. fierce		
13. funny		
14. wise		
15. smart		

Bonus Write a paragraph using four words you added from the chart above.

_____

_____

_____

_____

_____

Prefixes and Suffixes

Directions: Read the words below. Write prefixes or suffixes on the lines next to them. Some spaces may be blank. Write the base or root word in the final column. You may need to add some letters.

	Prefix	Suffix	Base or Root Word
1. bicycle	_____	_____	_____
2. careless	_____	_____	_____
3. creation	_____	_____	_____
4. discover	_____	_____	_____
5. enjoy	_____	_____	_____
6. friendly	_____	_____	_____
7. happiness	_____	_____	_____
8. hopeful	_____	_____	_____
9. joyful	_____	_____	_____
10. kindness	_____	_____	_____
11. nonfat	_____	_____	_____
12. redo	_____	_____	_____
13. resending	_____	_____	_____
14. untied	_____	_____	_____

Directions: Look in a book or around your classroom to find three words with prefixes, three words with suffixes, and three words with both prefixes and suffixes. Write them in the chart below.

Prefixes	Suffixes	Both

Ways a Word Can Grow

Quick Lesson—each prefix and suffix attached to a word can change its meaning.

Directions: Form new words by attaching different prefixes and suffixes to the words below. Add to each web as needed.

1. live

2. create

3. compute

4. tie

5. love

6. turn

Words Can Grow

Directions: Chose a base or a root word and attach different prefixes and suffixes to make new words. Add to each web as needed.

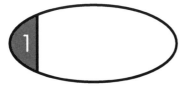

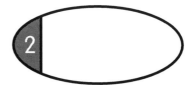

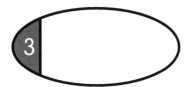

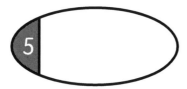

Make a Word Game

Teacher Directions: Print sets of prefix, suffix, and base word cards for each student or group. If possible, print the three sets on different-colored paper in order to reinforce the concepts of prefixes, suffixes, and base words. Have students cut out the sets of cards and arrange them face-up on a table. Have students combine cards to create new words. Advanced students can be asked to write the words they make and show the changes the word might undergo, such as dropping a silent **e**, changing a **y** to an **i**, or adding a double consonant.

co- | write

Prefixes

bi-	co-	con-
de-	dis-	em-
en-	ex-	im-
in-	mis-	out-
pre-	re-	sub-
trans-	un-	under-

Make a Word Game (cont.)

Suffixes

-able	-er	-or
-d	-ed	-en
-n	-est	-st
-ful	-ing	-less
-ly	-ment	-ness
-r	-er	-s
-es	-tion	-y

Make a Word Game (cont.)

Base Words

act	agree	bright
cycle	comfort	dance
elect	happy	hope
port	power	push
rough	side	tire
tract	use	view
wish	wonder	work

Answer Key

Page 5
1. arrange
2. glide
3. mural
4. observe
5. recall
6. passage
7. perform
8. vine
9. plan
10. point
11. print
12. publish
13. confine
14. consider
15. continent

Bonus: Look at the fourth letter to compare order.

Page 6
Answers will vary.

Page 8
1. cookbook
2. notebook
3. scrapbook
4. storybook
5. textbook
6. workbook
7. yearbook

Stories will vary.

Pages 9–10
Possible compound words:
afternoon, bathhouse, bathtub, beehive, birdbath, birdhouse, blueberry, bluebird, boathouse, bookcase, butterfly, buttermilk, cookbook, dogfish, doghouse, flypaper, football, goldfish, handball, handshake, honeybee, houseboat, inside, instep, lifeboat, lifeguard, milkshake, notebook, outboard, outhouse, outline, outside, playroom, playhouse, sandbox, sandpaper, scrapbook, skateboard, storyboard, storybook, strawberry, textbook, workday, workout

Page 13
1. dis—not; opposite
2. mis—wrongly
3. pre—before
4. un—not
5. em—cause to
6. re—again
7. en—cause to
8. im—not
9. non—without; not

Page 14
1. cocaptain
2. cooperate
3. copilot
4. coworker
5. cowrite
6–10. Answers will vary.

Page 15
1. deactivate; to make inactive
2. defrost; to release from a frozen state
3. deice; to remove ice from
4. deplane; to get out of an airplane after it lands
5. depress; to press something down
6. deice
7. deplane
8. depress
9. defrost
10. deactivate

Bonus: Check sentences for understanding.

Page 16
Down	Across
1. disappear	5. dislike
2. disorder	6. discontinue
3. disagree	7. disobey
4. dishonest	

Page 17
1. hug
2. to like something
3. enable—help to do something
4. endanger—put in danger; cause to be in danger
5. enlarge—make bigger; cause to be bigger
6. enrich—cause to be better or richer
7. entangle—tangle up; cause to be tangled
8. enjoy—cause to get pleasure or happiness

Bonus: Empower means to give power. Sentences will vary.

Page 18
1. rude
2. very difficult
3. not doing anything
4. not finished; partly done
5. wrong; having errors
6. cheap
7. not able to be seen
8–14. Answers will vary.

Page 19
1. mislead—to lead in the wrong direction
2. misspell—to spell incorrectly
3. mistake—to be wrong; to choose incorrectly
4. misunderstand—to understand incorrectly
5. misuse—to use incorrectly
6. misplace—to put something in the wrong place
7. mislead
8. misplace
9. misspell
10. misunderstand
11. misuse
12. mistake

Bonus: Answers will vary.

Page 20
1. not living
2. will not stick to things
3. not made with milk
4. not human
5. having no fat
6. (un)fair
7. (un)happy
8. (un)broken
9. (un)known
10. (un)locked

Sentences will vary.

Page 21
1. preboard
2. preorder
3. predict
4. preschool
5. prevent
6. after
7. after
8. before
9. before
10. before

Page 22
1. rebuild—to build or create something again
2. recycle—to process old items to make new items
3. reduce—to make smaller
4. research—to find out more about something
5. refuse—to say you will not do something
6. reuse—to use something again
7. rewrite—to write something again
8. reduce
9. recycle
10. reuse

Bonus: Drawings will vary.

Page 23
1. telegram—a message sent from far away by telegraph
2. telegraph—an old way to send messages from far away using wires
3. telephone—a device that sends voices over long distances
4. telephoto lens—a large lens to take pictures of things far way
5. telescope—an instrument used to view objects far away
6. television—an electronic system to transmit pictures and sound

Bonus: Answers will vary.

Answer Key *(cont.)*

Page 24

1. mis
2. pre
3. re
4. re
5. mis
6. re
7. un
8. un
9. un
10. pre

Bonus: Cross out these words: delock, unwake, and deschool

Page 25

1. non; not fiction, about facts
2. un; not happy
3. in; not active
4. un; not caring
5. in; ex; from the outside
6. dis; to stop being visible
7. ex; dis; to make something not be able to work
8. un; to remove a cover from

Bonus: Check answers for understanding.

Page 26

1–11. Check definitions for accuracy.

Page 27

Answers will vary.

Page 28

1–6. Answers will vary.
7. not special, no value
8. not ordinary
9. not being respectful
10. cannot be done

Page 30

First word(s) listed should be circled:

1. three; triceratops
2. eight; octagon
3. one hundred; century
4. one; unicorn
5. thousand; millennium
6. eight; octopus
7. ten; decade
8. pair; Binoculars
9. Elsa and her two/three sisters, triplets
10. two; bicycle

Bonus: 4 quadrilateral; 6 hexagon; 8 octagon; 5 pentagon

Page 31

1. 5 – quintet
2. 2 – duo
3. 4 – quartet
4. 3 – trio
5. 6 – sextet

Bonus: duet

Page 32

1. bicycle
2. octagon
3. quarter
4. triangle
5. hexagon
6. binoculars
7. octopus
8. unicorn
9. tricycle
10. triplets
11. Triceratops
12. unicycle

Page 34

Examples will vary.

1. more than one
2. without
3. full of
4. able to be
5. comparing most
6. something that
7. currently doing
8. done in the past
9. a completed action
10. someone who
11. someone who
12. state of being

Page 35

1. -cian; someone who
2. -ing; currently doing
3. -less; without
4. -tion, -sion; something that
5. -ly; how something is done
6. -ness; state of being
7. -or, -er, -ar; someone who
8. -n, -en; show a completed action
9. -able; able to be
10. -ment; state of being

Page 36

1. er   teacher
2. or   actor
3. er   singer
4. or   collector
5. or   sculptor
6. er   dancer
7. er   printer
8. or   director
9. ar   beggar
10. or   instructor

Check sentences for understanding.

Bonus: scholar—someone who knows a lot about a particular subject

Page 37

1. decayed
2. dozed
3. grinned
4. absorbed
5. paused
6. starved
7. supplied
8. untied

Page 38

1. awaken
2. broken
3. stolen
4. taken
5. lengthen
6. moisten
7. sharpen
8. shorten
9. whiten
10. sweeten
11. golden
12. wooden
13. woolen
14. strengthen
15. loosen

Check sentences for understanding.

Page 39

1. colorful
2. hopeful
3. armful
4. playful
5. careful
6. helpful
7. scoopful
8. mouthful
9. joyful

Page 40

1. playing
2. touching
3. smelling
4. running
5. waiting
6. thinking
7. tasting
8. locating
9. untying
10. lying

Page 41

1. harmless; harm; less; without harm
2. fearless; fear; less; without fear
3. thoughtless; thought; less; without thought
4. speechless; speech; less; without speech
5. thankless; thank; less; without thanks
6. worthless; worth; less; without worth
7. useless; use; less; without use
8. hopeless; hope; less; without hope
9. fearless
10. speechless
11. flightless
12. helpless

Page 42

1. anxiously
2. generously
3. cautiously
4. mysteriously
5. grumpily
6. slowly
7. easily
8. curiously
9. angrily

Definitions and sentences will vary.

Bonus: Answers will vary.

Page 43

1. amazement
2. enjoyment
3. movement
4. improvement
5. enlargement
6. treatment
7. enlargement
8. improvement
9. movement
10. amazement
11. treatment
12. enjoyment

Bonus:

Page 44

1. dryness—wetness
2. sadness—happiness
3. fullness—emptiness
4. hopelessness—hopefulness
5. silliness
6. goofiness
7. kindness
8. friendliness
9. happiness
10. fairness
11. sweetness
12. cheerfulness
13. grumpiness
14. ugliness

Bonus: Answers will vary.

Answer Key (cont.)

Page 45
1. decision—*de* dropped
2. conclusion—*de* dropped
3. revision—*se* dropped
4. discussion—*s* dropped
5. admission—*t* changed to *s*
6. connection
7. direction
8. election
9. education
10. illustration
11. imitation

Page 46
1. noun; adjective; verb
2. noun; noun; adjective
3. noun/verb; verb; adjective
4. verb; adjective; adjective
5. verb; adjective; verb
Bonus: Possible answers:
   Noun: water + s = waters
   Verb: water + ing/ed/s =
   watering/watered/waters
   Adjective: water + y = watery

Page 47
1. useless
2. lively
3. shameless
4. tasteless
5. hopeful
6. wasteful
7. peaceful
8. fortunately
9. pasted
10. mistaken
11. driver
12. looser
13. wisest
14. grading
15. writing
16. closest

Page 48

Suffix	-ed	-er	-ful	-less	-ly
call	called	caller			
dance	danced	dancer			
happy		happier			happily
help	helped	helper	helpful	helpless	helpfully
hope	hoped		hopeful	hopeless	hopefully
smile	smiled	smiler		smileless	smiley

1. present
2. present
3. future
4. past
5. present
6. past
7. past
8. past
9. happyness
10. runing
11. disslike
12. peacefull
13. directtion
14. easyly

Page 49
1. fairy; fairies
2. cherry; cherries
3. baby; babies
4. puppy; puppies
5. study; studies
6. blackberry; blackberries
7. strawberry
8. city
9. penny
10. flies
11. cherries
12. puppies

Page 50
1. patios
2. stereos
3. igloos
4. radios
5. buffaloes
6. potatoes
7. tomatoes
8. volcanoes
Add -s: autos, memos, studios, zeros, zoos
Add -es: echoes, heroes, vetoes

Page 51
1. axes
2. buses
3. foxes
4. dishes
5. sandwiches
6. scarves
7. elves
8. wolves
9. leaves
10. lives
11. shelves
12. staffs
13. safes
14. chefs
15. reefs

Page 52
1. wishes
2. diaries
3. calves
4. potatoes
5. houses
6. rodeos
7. stories
8. fables
9. ranches
10. shelves
11. pianos
12. buses
13. countries
14. volcanoes
15. days
16. sprouts
17. videos
18. loaves
19. tooth—teeth
20. mouse—mice
21. child—children
22. goose—geese
23. ox—oxen
24. man—men

Page 53
1. tall, taller; small, smaller; big, bigger
2. long, longer; short, shorter
3. small, smaller; big, bigger
Bonus: Check comparisons for accuracy.

Page 54
1. largest
2. greenest
3. coldest
4. wisest
5. spicier; spiciest
6. saltier; saltiest
7. friendlier; friendliest
8. flatter; flattest
9. sadder; saddest
10. slimmer; slimmest

Page 55
1. frailer; frailest
2. harsher; harshest
3. scarier; scariest
4. simpler; simplest
5. briefer; briefest
6. riskier; riskiest
7. swifter; swiftest
8. easier; easiest
9. chillier; chilliest
10. harder; hardest
11. slimier; slimiest
12. fiercer; fiercest
13. funnier; funniest
14. wiser; wisest
15. smarter; smartest
Bonus: Answers will vary.

Page 56

	Prefix	Suffix	Base or Root Word
1.	bi		cycle
2.		less	care
3.		tion	create
4.	dis		cover
5.	en		joy
6.		ly	friend
7.		ness	happy
8.		ful	hope
9.		ful	joy
10.		ness	kind
11.	non		fat
12.	re		do
13.	re	ing	send
14.	un	d	tie

Bonus: Answers will vary.

Page 57
Suggested answers, but others are possible:
1. lives, lived, living, lively, liven, livelier, liveliest, enliven
2. created, creation, creating, creator, creates, recreate, recreates, recreation, recreating, recreated
3. computed, computes, computer, computing
4. untie, retie, tied, tying, ties
5. lovely, loving, lover, loved, loves, lovelier, loveliest
6. turns, turned, turning, return, overturn, turner

Page 58
Answers will vary.

Pages 59–61
Answers will vary.

Made in the USA
Columbia, SC
06 August 2020